THE DEMOCRAT BLUE WAVE IS THE 2ND ALAMO

Turning Texas Liberal in the 2020 Presidential Election

T. H. Logwood

"Remember the Alamo"

TEXAS IS UNDER ATTACK

"War is upon us!" Just like in the early 1800's when Texas was just a territory, an invasion was taking place. It was a time when the American settlers were moving into the new lands of what is now broad and massive Texas. Then, the territory already populated (granted somewhat sparsely), by tribes of native peoples and Mexican nationals, and ever increasing numbers of "Gringos" seeking a better life and new opportunities. That is part of the American story, the story of our expanding nation, but many saw the newcomers as invaders, looking to change the status quo.

Then at some point, tensions rose to conflict, which escalated, which then became the full blown Texan revolution. The pinnacle of course is the famous Battle of the Alamo. The result was of course, the Republic of Texas, and later the State o Texas. What occurred was a cultural upheaval (of sorts), whereby more "American" values took place of whatever societal norms there were in Old Texas. Not that one way of living was better or lesser than the other, but the point is a general shift happened because of the influx of new comers into the territory.

Remember the Alamo? Or was that erased from history because it's "racist" or somebody got their feelings hurt, type of political correctness lunacy? It was a fight for survival, then for the emerging new Republic, now, for Texas and the country as a whole. What is interesting, is a parallel between then and now, where the influx of new citizens gradually, and then abruptly, made a major change in the society.

What makes Texas and Texans different than the rest of America? Everything! Texas is the bastion of American values and traditions. They stand fast to the southern principles of family, community, hard work, limited government, free expression, reverence for God, Life at conception, individualism, and self defense. These are Texan values, Southern values, and traditional American values. And they are threatened.

The next election, the 2020 Presidential battle, may very well favor the democrat candidates, threatening every tradition and value long-held dear. With each election cycle, more and more new citizens move into Texas. Many of these people are democrat activists, highly motivated and well-funded party workers seeking to change everything Texas. Not that democrats are bad, or vermin to eradicate, but many that come and settle here have a nefarious agenda. As the new focus of the democrat party has evolved into what is called, the "radical left wing", or "socialist left", their values are being promoted and pushed throughout the Texan territory.

Over the last several election cycles, like the 2018 mid-terms, it was clear how deeply embedded the democrats are in the major cities like Houston, El Paso, and San Antonio. These areas used to be solidly traditional Texan, now changed. This infiltration touts policies and ideas that conflict with the mainstream traditions of most Texans.

The new democrat party promotes an "open door" stance in regards to borders and immigration, government oversight of religious values, control of education, a government sponsored health care system, highly restrictive gun ownership (if not outright confiscation), and a crackdown on freedom of expression. They encourage government programs to take care of every need, including income equality. They elevate the status of illegal immigrants, including the criminals and child-slavery bondsmen, over legal and natural Texas (American) citizens. Life of the unborn has no rights. The new party promises higher wages via the redistribution of wealth, and taxing the evil rich (white) aristocracy. Look at the changes in the major cities over the last several decades. Is this what Texans want from there governing bodies?

The radical wing uses slogans and bold words to promote their beliefs. "Be tolerant of other people and their lifestyles." "Save the planet by ending fossil fuels." "The government is your family, your provider, and your god." The bottom line is, they want a government controlled socialist Texas. The decisions and policies for the people, made by an elite group of "honorable and intelligent" leaders, as they know best how to govern Texas (and the nation. They promise the "good life", without the worry of consequence. Research and learn for yourself, who and what the new democrat party really stands for, but they do not stand for Texan values.

Wake up Texas. Wake up America. The invaders are here. Over the past decade or so, some of these new residents are party activists trying to push the democrat mindset, which are not in our best interests. These activists are scattered throughout the state, in areas where the democrat voter base is increasing, particularly among the newer naturalized citizens. They have become more active around pockets of younger voters, such as the campuses in the larger cities. They are pushing into the heartland of traditionally republican counties and districts, seeking to sway voters into "progressive thinking".

FLIPPING TEXAS RED TO BLUE

"Texas is a conservative Republican Red state, always has been, always will be." Really? How about not really. Looking at the data of election results from the Texas State Elections Commission, the state flipped back and forth between Red and Blue over the years. This is true among the districts, governorship, and of course the presidential elections.

Texas - 1964 v. 2016 Presidential Elections

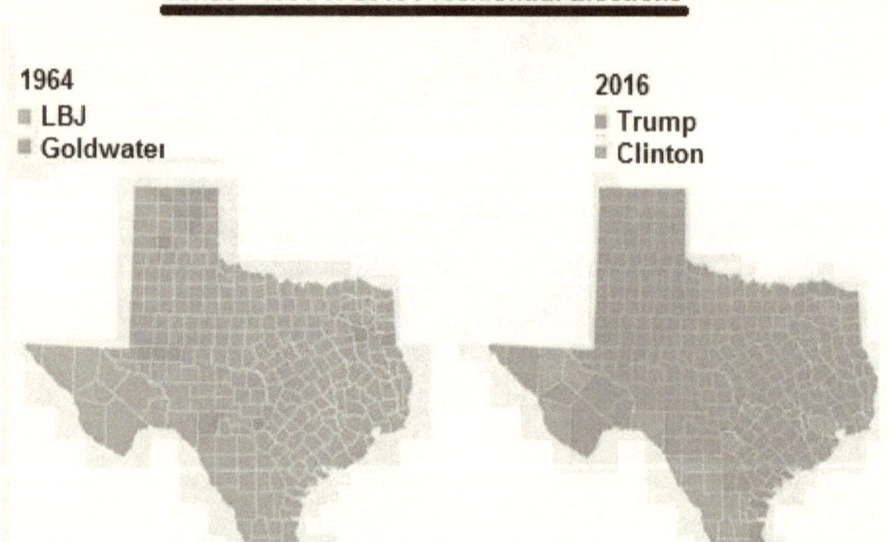

But when looking just at the presidential races from 1960 to 2016, there are a couple interesting thoughts to consider. During 1960, 1964, and 1968, Texas was Democrat Blue. The electoral votes for the state went for JFK, LBJ, and Humphrey, respectively. These were the ol' stalwarts of the Democrat Party, the working-man's party, the leaders we loved and respected. Their policies and traditions, lined up with those held by Texans.

Then the Nixon era flipped the state Red in 1972, and would have remained Red, but Texas sided with Carter during the 1976 election. Perhaps in part because of the controversies surrounding the administration. Or perhaps because Carter was an southern agrarian that held values closer to mainstream Texans at the time. Then came along Reagan.

It was said that Ronald Reagan was Texan at heart, and that some swear he was San Antonio born and raised. Certainly he held the same beliefs and values that Texans, and most Americans held. The Reagan era flipped Texas Red, and has remained Red ever since. The point is that it has been the core values and traditions that most Texans held close that moved the state one direction or the other. Texas can flip Blue, sure it can, just depends on who shows up to the polls. The democrats run a well-oiled machine that gets the vote out, and changes do happen.

During this same time period, California and Colorado had been staunch Republican held territories since 1960. In 1964, both sided with LBJ, but otherwise the votes favored the republicans since 1968. In 1992, both states sided with Clinton. California, the hard-core conservative Reagan republican stronghold, once thought forever Red, flipped in 1992, and has been democrat Blue ever since. Colorado went Red for Dole and the Bush era, but flipped Blue with Obama in 2008, and has remained democrat held. It was believed that Colorado could never be flipped as it was in the Red mid-western block. Beliefs and values change, but it depends who votes, and the how motivated people are in voting that can flip a state. As noted, the democrats work hard to get the vote out.

Growing up as a Kennedy-era Democrat, I too held what I thought were reasonable ideas. I was raised believing in "the process", discussion and debate, fairness and kindness, making ideas into plans that helped the working man and others. Like my father, and his father before him, it was reasonable to follow the parties' principles of making positive changes for the country. That was a time when disagreement led to discussion and reason, ending in comprised outcomes that benefited the whole. Not any more. The old democrat party is gone (or dead silent), and the new party is all about radical ideas that benefits only a small elite class.

The new democrat party aligns itself to bold speech with no substance. They use violence and the mob to enact change. They use divisive rhetoric to stir up the masses of brainwashed zombies to overthrow society, on every issue of tradition, law, and freedoms. The new party professes the goodness of socialistic ideals, but whitewashes the realities of repeated historical failures. Condemnation without solution. The peoples party is no longer the party of the people, but by the elitists pushing to overturn the rights of free speech, rule of law, equality for all. The are indoctrinating of our school children with the idea that "government provides", versus hard work and achievement by merit.

This radical departure of party norms relates exactly to every election, where more and more districts and States are turning blue. Turning blue, not by advancing sound policies and programs to make positive changes (as they offer none), but more so accomplished through unrealistic ideals. The general populace is being brainwashed by empty rhetoric that touts restriction and control, unsubstantiated emotional opinion over logic and reason. Yet the vote turns blue, more and more often. It's like in the movies, when the people change from normal to zombies, and the power of the individual is given over to mass hysteria (the mob mentality).

If this country is to be changed, let it be changed through the process of law as it was founded. But what is changed, may not be what is good or right, or even fair. And what changes, is not easily changed back. If traditions are deemed wrong, and what we have previously known as failed ideologies become entrenched, then individual liberties are restricted. The rule of law becomes mute, contrary to those established by our forefathers, and power becomes concentrated in the hands of a few. It's happening across Texas, and throughout the nation.

Who, or what groups adhere to what you hold as good and right? What you believe in, and the rights and privileges you enjoy, are just a few votes away from being changed. Think for yourself, and decide in the way that works best for you. Align yourself with those that hold those principles and ideals you want.

THE CALIFORNICATION OF TEXAS

The 2018 mid-term election is over, and Senator Ted Cruz was re-elected, but not by much. The State of Texas remains Republican Red, for now. "Texas is Red, always has been Red, and will always remain Red". Or will it? The democrat plan is to turn Texas into California, with its strong central government, high taxation, social services to everyone, with a wide open border along the Rio Grande

Under Ronald Reagan, California was conservative, the bastion of economic progress and prosperity, relatively low taxes, and a role model for the rest of the country. After the Reagan era, California had a couple more republican governors, but not great leaders, and the democrats became clever in their candidates. Slowly they gained seats and increased their prowess until they gained the governorship.

And look at the state today, a toilet, full of filth and corruption, and led by socialists. Crime is horrible, the police are hand-cuffed by mayors lacking to protect the people or property, and homeless bums and illegal aliens prowl without control. In San Francisco, once the jewel of California, Nancy Pelosi allowed drugs and gangs to pollute the streets, while she sits comfortably in her walled penthouse palace with her armed guards. The economy is bolstered only by the hi tech companies that fill Silicon Valley. The roads are degrading, regulations and high taxes have weakened the economy to the point where companies are leaving the state. The cost of living has become very high, partly due to regulations and taxes, and home ownership is completely unafford-able. The rub is, that it does not have to be like that. It was a great state before, but under better management.

Just because what was, should never imply that something will remain. Pride or delusion can be a strong drink, but the truths and realities of this world have a sneaky way of catching even the best of people off guard. The results of the 2018 Texas mid-term elections was alarming from the perspective that democrat turnout was very high. "Beto" was very close to winning, not because of his merits and experiences as a leader, but rather from the democrat marketing campaign that promoted him.

Traditional Texas influences on voters, like jobs, economy, and so on, are no longer the driving principles many voter segments care about. If so, with the great economic rebound, the successes President Trump has had (despite the media lies), one would forecast that republicans should have won by vast margins in the 2018 election cycle. Just not so, the wins were marginal. Depending on the voter group or segment, they care about different optics. Whether it is of hyped rhetoric, or emotional dribble and fear, many groups vote based on superficial perceptions. Facts and realities don't assure votes any longer.

Throughout the state, especially strong democrat voter participation pushed many races very close to victory. The newcomers into the state, the democrat activists, have been working or years to get people excited about thinking and voting differently. Winning by a few percentage points should comfort no one, because the next race, they will be even more prepared. The democrat marketing machine is well funded and highly effective in reaching the voter. They will flip Texas. "As Texas goes, so goes the country (following the California model)".

With greater democrat influence in the state, the traditional Texas values of family, strong faith, independence from government control, staunch patriotism, the robust economy, and independent pride, are changing. The changes could usher in a new era of thinking. The great media hype of a Democrat "Blue Wave" did in fact happen, and it almost worked in Texas. The goal and machinery to flip Texas Blue is in place. 2018 was a practice campaign for the 2020 election. The reality is that Texas could become the next California, and in just a very short time from now.

Is that true? Laughable and crazy as that sounds, consider this, California was the cornerstone of conservatism, proud and strong, with an economy of its' own about 5th in world prowess. Under the governorship of then Ronald Reagan, California was a golden prize of strength and economic prosperity. Now look at the state, it's a sniveling bastion of government controlled, poverty stricken, handout dependent mess. Crime is ever increasing, drug gangs and homeless bums control the streets in many cities, taxes are through the roof, government fraud and waste are rampant, with a total lack of godliness or value for life. The big cities are a mess. Sure, the state has the mighty hi-tech industry, a cornucopia of agriculture, and has the San Francisco hub of corporate headquarters, but it's a skeleton of its former self.

California was Red, always has been Red, and was believed to always remain Red. Now look at it, Blue. It has been Blue since Jerry Brown and the democrats took over in the early 1990's, and will always remain Blue. Consider California now. People are leaving the state in droves, as illegal immigrants flood across the border and suck on the public programs intended for citizens. Do we want that for Texas?

Now what is so wrong and bad about Democrat Blue? "That is a biased and 'racist' statement. Only a dumb mid-western redneck would say such things, obviously a degenerate deplorable Republican. Californians are beautiful people. What difference does it make if a state is Blue or Red, democrat or republican, that's just politics. At the end of the day, people are just trying to get through the day, free to do their own thing. Who should care which political party is in office, it has nothing to do with daily life." What? Who should care? All of us.

That is the whole point, it makes all a difference! It makes a difference who leads us, the values and principles our leaders have, and how every aspect of our daily lives are influenced by governmental policy. All of that matters to Texans. To what point can or should government dictate what "we the people" should, do, think, or act? How is it, that a select group of leaders, rule over how we regulate our family values and beliefs? What we do to provide for our loved ones, and what is acceptable to say or think about life is not the role of government. That is not Texan, and that is not solid American ideology.

Remember the Alamo? Or was that erased from the "white supremacist" history books also? "We don't want to offend anybody, it is not fair to talk about so and so, or such a group, or talk about such mean and hateful things". Wake up Texas. Wake up America. Hollywood morals, and San Francisco habits are invading the Lone Star State. They are here! It is very true, very real, and the 2020 election could be very telling. Should Texas go Blue, then there will never be another conservative or Republican elected to Washington again. What Texans traditionally have believed and have been, will be replaced by the weak government-centered ideology that has ruined California, Colorado, New York, the New England states, and soon Texas. "Defend the Alamo, they are coming back". The invaders want to evolve the Texas Republic into a "more tolerant kinder place" (at the expense of your rights and pocketbook).

Consider this, the 2018 mid-term election was an invasion of Texas. The Blue Wave "did" happen, the flood of Democrat-minded influence was huge, and was close to flipping the state. However, that was Not the goal of the Democrats for that election cycle, it was a test-run. It was a trial run for the 2020 election, but nearly flipped Texas anyways. Senator Ted Cruz defeated the Democrat opponent, Robert "Beto" O'Rourke, but only by less than 3%. That was not a mandate of Texas values, nor a comforting margin to think that Red will remain Red.

No, it was the just the opposite. The reality is that it was too close, and nearly a surprise disaster the oblivious Republican Party. According to the news and information about the election, the Cruz campaign had about 20 staff people (statewide), whereas the "Beto" staff had nearly 800 people working statewide! The Democrats spent something like $70 million dollars on a political campaign that almost worked. Whether the numbers are correct or not, the point is that the Democrats want Texas, and they are investing long-term for it. It was not planned to be successful for the 2018 election, it was "planted", like weed-seeds, to grow and fester, to choke out the Reds, next time. For months, and actually years, the democrats have been pouring in money, activist supporters, growing their influence in every county of Texas. The 2018 election was not the end, just part of the growing process.

The democrat strategy of gradually influencing and taking over a state is brilliant. They are a team, well funded, not from within the prospective target state, but from their bases (states) of strength, like California. The Democrats are funded from Hollywood elitists, large corporate and private donors, such as George Sorros (through the organizations he controls), according to news sources. This is what happened in California, the gradual build up of Blue resources, and the state flipped. It happened in Colorado, forever believed to be Red. Then "whamo", turned Blue in 1992, and has been Blue ever since. And how well has Colorado fared since then? And look at Colorado now, it's falling apart. They have a long-term strategy of investing time, money, and influence in every state, little by little, with each election, the Democrats are picking off the clueless Red districts and entire states.

What the "Peoples Party" wants, is to turn Texas into California. Its called "Californication". How well has California done over the past 20 years? Managed by corrupt socialist bureaucrats, supported and promoted by Hollywood elitists and a biased media, California has seen a total meltdown of everything good the Reagan-era Republicans had built. Taxes are ever increasing, businesses (except for the hi-tech giants that support the agenda) are leaving the state every day. Regulations are strangling every industry and company trying to pay the bills. The infrastructure is in decay, and costs ever more to maintain the potholes and contractual bribes to certain politicians. People, particularly the Caucasian late-middle to retiree segment, are fleeing to less costly states. At the same time, illegal immigrants are welcomed with government assistance programs to "take care of" the new citizens (at taxpayer expense).

There are so many Californicated debacles to mention, but just listen to any reputable media about the graft and corruption for yourselves. A couple that are notable include the hi-speed bullet train to nowhere. A super train-rail system intended to ease traffic and air pollutants from Sacramento to San Francisco, not even started, already billions in the red. Supported by federal matching funds (our federal tax dollars from our paychecks), the poor taxpayers are funding yet another Jerry Brown boondoggle government-mandated program. The people didn't want the project, they wanted to see improved water development for farmers to grow food. But huge special interest groups lobbied, pushed, and bribed their way into getting the project underway. And naturally, the politicians jumped on board.

In Santa Barbara County, Reagan's' former home turf, the city council approved a ban on plastic straws to help save the planet. The council, not the voters, decided that plastic straws are destroying the ocean life, so criminal fines and jail time are imposed on offenders. Restaurants, stores, and the private individual would be persecuted as criminals for their hennas possessions and solicitations. Yet, criminal and drug-related offenders are allowed to roam the streets less harassed, because of limited law enforcement budgets. It's not known if the State has yet approved that as a state-wide ban, but that would be par for the course.

In Monterey County, California, a wealthy now touristy and

Hollywood retirement Mecca, the town of Pacific Palisades won't allow traditional 4th of July celebration, because it is offensive to certain groups (namely the city council). Rather, on July 4th, they commemorate a Chinese festival.

Similarly, under the Governor Brown controlled government, the whole illegal immigrant problem has been one of defiance to federal law. Illegal aliens crossing the border have been given "special citizenry" status for years, made even more valued than the native or naturalized people since the Trump presidency began in early 2017. Not only had several of the larger cities, San Francisco, Los Angeles, and maybe Sacramento, declared themselves as "sanctuary cities", but Brown had declared that California was a "sanctuary state". In open rebellion of federal law to protect American citizens from known criminals, who were in the country illegally, California embraces them, and offers "safe haven" to all illegals. The dishonesty of state lawyers and politicians, have twisted "the rule of law" to the harm of the general populace. Their underlying motives are monetary gain and influence.

The list of California government imposed rules and laws are not always for the good of the people, nor honestly approved by the voter. The deceptive wording of the ballot propositions, promoted to voters by the biased media and special interests, have hidden the realities of many legislative actions. The bulk of Californians are good hard working regular people trying to do the best they can in this life, with the bulk of the voting populace is in the major cities. The cities are a disaster zone, ruled by entrenched politicians, but the rural areas tend to hold more of the former republican traditions. The honest voice of the masses is under represented, as the major cities dictate election outcomes.

How about San Francisco, once the jewel of the California, is now a cesspool where human feces and drug needles line the streets, and homeless bums prowl around like animals. This is a district controlled by the majority leader in the House, Nancy Pelosi, that professes helping the poor and homeless, fighting big business, and defying the evils of the president. That woman is a liar and hypocrite in the worst way. How many illegal immigrant families live in her high-rise walled penthouse palace, protected by armed guards? What has she done to help the people that elected her? Hmm, wait, she's not there. She is too busy flying democrat colleagues around the world as "public relations" trips (at tax payer expense). Instead of helping to resolve the national security and border wall issue, she disregards American safety and federal laws, while embracing the influx of harmful activities along our southern border. Why help illegals? Because they are groomed to vote democrat. It's all about the power and influence, and lots of taxpayer money.

One can research for themselves to learn of the numerous messes befalling California. It is all caused from governmental mismanagement and wacky philosophies. This is what will happen to Texas. Turning Texas Blue, means Texas becoming "California II".

The end game is this, not just control over Texas, but a democrat controlled Washington, forever. The new democrat platform values government-sponsored, government-influenced, government control, of every aspect of American life. In other words, a socialist America. The current democrat party is no longer the party of the "working man", but is wrought with socialist ideals of government dependence and influence over the masses.

A BLUE TEXAS

Just recall the Obama/Biden era, eight years of governmental regulations, weak and decimated business and economic free-fall. They enacted ever increasing taxes that drained your hard-earned resources, government failure to provide the promised health care, weak and disrespected influence worldwide, and division between the diversity of peoples that make up America. Rights and freedoms ever more restricted, like with guns, free speech, and even (Christian) worship. They were saving the planet by nearly destroying the coal and oil industries. The Obama/Biden era is just a foreshadow of the things to come, a weak government-controlled socialist state.

A Blue Texas will look much different than what we know of Texas today. Guns? Nope, gone. Either taken away, or heavily taxed or restricted by ever increasing limitations. If you even mention a firearm, and the "Red Flag" laws will arrest you and confiscate your property, contrary to our constitutional Rights. Health Care: a one-payer system, controlled by inept bureaucrats, typified by high insurance premiums and poor service (sound familiar?). How about the new Texas Green Economy? Oil is out, shut down or heavily regulated, because "it causes global-warming and melting of the icecaps in Antarctica". Rather, power will be supplied by Chinese-made solar panels, and wind mills, fueled by government-belching wind. No more cattle. "Cattle waste causes evil greenhouse gases", and "red meat is racist". Rather than livestock, broccoli fields will replace stockyards, harvested by the exaggerated mass migrations of "new citizenry" sanctioned and protected by new government "sanctuary mandates".

Taxes, no problem, "give the government everything you make, and they will take care of you". "Life in the womb isn't life, it can be discarded like trash". And don't be concerned about educating your children, "they" will take care of that, starting with the rewriting of Texas history. "The Alamo wasn't about defense of the new republic", but rather it may reverberate "the woes of the poor oppressed people that lived in the territory, and the evil Texans and American conspirators stole it". Shall I go on?

If Texas were to become a democrat-controlled state, then it may as well be called the "Peoples State of California II". If the democrats were of the ol' Kennedy or even LBJ era, fine, but the reality is quite the contrary. Look what's happening across this country, and learn for yourselves what Texas can become.

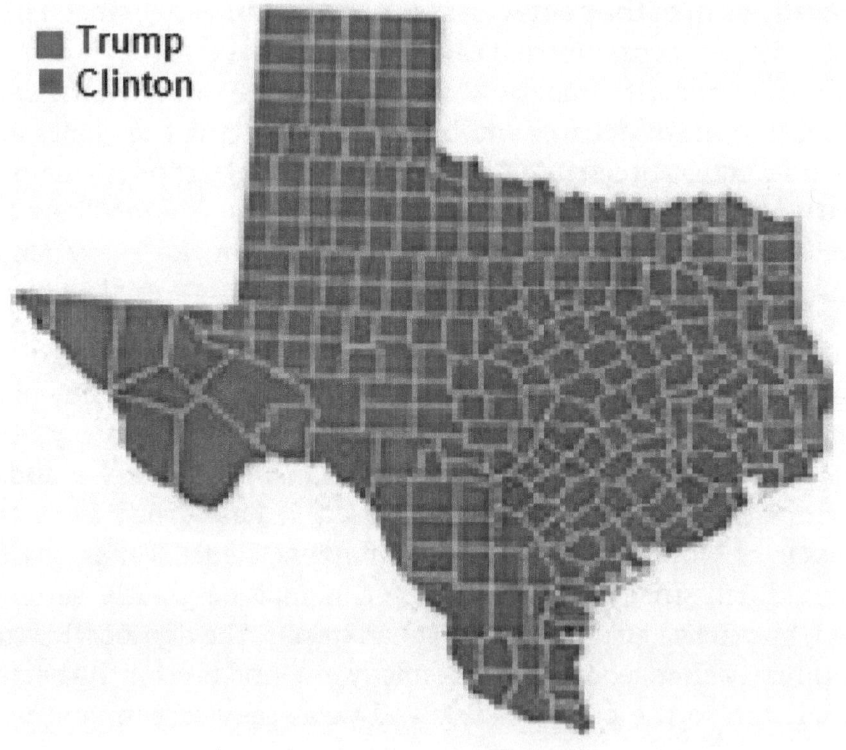

RED TEXAS

The 2018 election cycle was not an anomaly, but a trend. Texas held most of the republican districts, but strong democrat turn-out made many races very close. Is it that what Texans believe or want? Or is it that the democrat voters were more passionate about voting? If the state is going to remain in one party's control or another, then the voters have to get active.

Rather than assess or describe a candidate, look at their voting records of how well they have handled the affairs of the people. How did each of the democrats (and the republicans), since 1980, deal with the economy and taxes, national sovereignty, and protection of the citizens. How well did each handle health care, education, immigration and borders, protecting the rights and freedoms guaranteed under the Constitution? Of those principles that you value, how did each of these candidates fare? These are questions that should be asked at every election, for every candidate, regardless of party affiliation.

The Clinton era started the downward spiral of the democrat party. With each successive candidate and leader, the party platform, their principles, have moved further and further away from main-stream democrats, and most Texans. With every scandal, corruption, and dirty laundry exposed, it has turned away the masses of would-be democrat supporters, hence Texas has remained Red since 1980. Certainly, this may be greatly generalized, but to the average voter, Texan or not, the democrat party has greatly changed from the Kennedy era. And not for the better. Just listen to the party leaders and what they scream and wail about? Do Texans want that?

Can Texas flip? Yes. Why or How? Voters can be swayed and convinced by the barrage of media and promises that candidates spew. The Kennedy-era generation is gone. Now the Millennial, the Generation-X, the younger voters are easily bamboozled by social media hype and fake biased news. The younger voter blocks are influenced by less than traditional values, and education indoctrination by social activist teachers. It is suggested that naturalized citizens, and minority groups, tend to favor the democrat candidates. Are they moved by candidate policies or promises, or fearful of repercussions or threats to their citizenship? Perhaps both, but perhaps more so, the democrat party voter outreach is a program of successful mass marketing. They reach out and follow up on interested voter prospects far better than any republican machine.

And the republican base is getting old. The ol' reliable republican base is changing, getting beyond voting age or ability, with poor outreach to the younger generation, or the new citizen bases. The republican public image is that of old tired white men, supported by big business, and the pursuit of wealth. Family values and tradition doesn't register with the younger voters, especially as the decline in marital commitments continues to plummet, leaving disenfranchised families. Naturalized voters fear the republicans will change laws that might threaten their citizenship. And the biased disgraceful main-stream media deflates any positives that republican leaders make, and exonerates the new democrat values over truth and impartiality.

LIARS, CHEATERS, AND HYPOCRITES

"Win at All Costs". Too often it seems to be the only way democrats can win is to cheat. The 2018 mid-term elections was wrought with manipulation and deceit, with the backing of main stream media, and powerful wealthy donors. The democrat party does not propose plans to improve the lives of people, but uses Gestapo-like tactics to quell any resistance, twist truths and news, and use the "mob" to intimidate and harass opposition. This is not the democratic party of JFK or even Bill Clinton. What was the welfare of the working man under the Kennedy era Democrats, which was the cornerstone of the party, has given way to radical socialistic dogma, with legions of brain-washed stooges to carry out mob violence and endless protests. Rather than come up with solutions to fix an issue, or make lives better for the people, they use rhetoric and hate speech, and the double standard to advance their dark agenda of seizing power.

What democrats scream and fuss about when republicans do something, they remain silent or praise those do the same against the republicans. Look at the spying and attempted coupe during the 2016 election, the lies of the Russian hoax, the Clinton scandals (including Bengazi), and Obama/Biden's arms deal to the Mexican drug cartels. Let's not forget the hundreds of millions of taxpayer dollars the Obama/Biden gave to Iran (supposedly in secret), or many briberies made by the Clintons and Biden. These are the tip of the iceberg that the democrats pull when in power. These are slowly being uncovered by the Trump administration and honest journalists. Yet, if a republican did anything like this, the media and democrats what throw a raging fit. There is a distinctive double-standard, or hypocrisy, demonstrated over and over again..

For example, President Trump and the border wall. The will of the people that elected Trump, want a border wall and increased security. It is fact that large amounts of drugs, crime, slavery, and masses of invading people, come across the southern border, half of which is in Texas. Most Americans want this invasion into our land to end. America is a sovereign nation that has the right to have a border and restrict people and activities from entering the country. This is also factual, and mandated in the US Constitution that the president has the right and authority to protect and enforce our national borders from outside influences (study Article 1 of the US Constitution). Bill Clinton argued and demanded a wall and protection along the border. Obama. Pelosi, Schumer, and many other democrats, as shown on video numerous times, citing the needs for border walls and security. Yet, because Trump is so greatly hated by most of the democrat leadership, the media, and their brain-washed masses, they all now oppose border security. For President Trump to succeed on this key election issue, the democrats would suffer greatly. Therefore, despite protecting Americans, our rights, our safety, they will oppose the wall until election day.

These elected officials are a disgrace and disgust that must not be tolerated. Politics, okay fine, but every delay tactic costs American lives, and so much more. Every public servant in given the "oath of office", whereby their pledge to uphold the law and the constitution. It is shameful, beyond shame what the democrats have done in recent years. These are the new democrats. Do we really want these types of leaders to control Texas, or the country?

Also because of the border wall struggle, the President has shut down a portion of the government to leverage pressure on the legislature to fund border security. Again, politics run the course, but increases the safety risks for the citizenry. Here again, Madame Pelosi, Speaker of the House, is suppose to bring about legislation and bills to become laws, but instead, she and many of her democrat colleagues are taking vacations to foreign countries (at taxpayer expense), instead of resolving the problem. She cries about spending and harm to the non-working federal employees, yet she is spending millions of public monies to play around the world. Hypocrisy is a bitter dish.

Using the "race card" at every opportunity to defame and defuse republican successes, the democrats slur people, insult and curse at opponents, use the same hate-filled rhetoric they claim the republicans spew. Without a morale compass, everything is fair game. At least, until the tables are turned onto themselves, where no condemnation is found.

Just like Ellis, the new leader of the DNC (Democratic National Committee), and a particular member of Congress, as well as others, cry foul at the Supreme Court Cavanaugh hearings with nothing but false accusations. Yet for these particular people, their own pasts are tainted with rape and woman abuse. This is fact, confirmed by books they have written, and interviews conducted, even confirmed on video with boastful comments.

On and on, there seems to be examples of prominent party leaders that profess one thing, yet do the opposite. Too many of them make promises, only to deny such upon gaining office. Granted, politics is an ugly business sometimes, and some candidates and elected people are morally corrupt, but that seems to be normal. The latest opinion polls suggests that President Trump has an approval rating of about 50 to 55%, and Congress about 12 to 14%. Whether accurate or not, the fact is that many people don't trust or like our elected leaders. Then vote them out. Learn about the candidates before they get into office, and join with those that are like-minded. Use your rights and freedoms to assemble, speak up, and then vote.

VOTER FRAUD - IT WINS ELECTIONS

Voter Fraud and Identity theft are on a national scale, according to many experts. This is one area where the democrats have opened up their bag of dirty tricks. Democrats? Yes, when has anyone ever heard of an election scandal involving republicans? The facts are there, check for yourself, it is always the democrats that are found with their "hands in the cookie jar" every time.

During the many voter registration drives the democrats do, many of the registration cards will ask for birth date, address, and last four numbers of the social security number. What for? As the Springfield, Missouri democratic office would reply, "for follow-up purposes". The scary part is that the personal information provided, is being sold or used, as an identity theft resource that can be used to fill voter registration boxes and vote tallies. This has been documented in numerous investigative reports.

If this is in fact true, then fake people can be set up as voters all across the country. If there is no voter ID laws in place, or with little to no verification, fraud, in the worst possible way can occur. Elections are then swayed, and illegitimate candidates have subverted our right to vote in our fair and free election system. "Fair and free", that is the premise and foundation of the laws for this country. And above all other nations, even throughout history, the idea and hope for elections that are not tampered with. Elections where candidates could make their case before the electorate, and in privacy the common citizen can cast their vote to freely to choose our leaders. Is that liberty slipping away?

At least four of the closest races of the 2018 mid-term elections, were contested by the democrat candidates, because of suspicious practices. But wait... "surprise surprise surprise", to quote Gomer Pyle from the famous TV show, magically, thousands of untallied ballots magically appeared "after" the final vote count. And surprisingly, "All" of the ballots were for the democratic candidate. In all of these cases, the "misplaced" ballots were 100% for the democratic party. Hmm, highly suspicious, as there is no way they are real. Statistically, that is impossible, at the very least. The only way democrats can win is to cheat. They have no policies or plans to excite the voter, so they have to resort to tricks and sneaky tactics.

In four of the highly reported races, those for the governor in Georgia, governor in Florida, senator in Texas, and also senator in Arizona, the results were contested. In each of these races, like in earlier campaigns, the republican candidate had won, but by a very small margin. Then "miracle ballots" magically appear, and have, or would have, pushed the democrat candidate over the top. This is fraud in the worst case.

In Arizona, signatures were not matching what was on record. Missing ballots suddenly appeared like "manna", and the rightful republican winner of the race had now lost. A recount produced the ever slightest victory for the democrat contender, no less a shame to every ideal we hold as fair and impartial elections.

In Broward County, Florida, Supervisor of Elections, Brenda Snipes, was again in the middle of the latest controversy. Suddenly after the election, when the democrat candidate lost the governors race, she (they) found thousands of missing ballots, all of which were for the democrat contender. In fact, and reported in many news reports, a legal expert was brought in to contest the election result for governor. As the race was very close, the democrats again sought to change the outcome. It was reported this lawyer touted that, "the election result will be turned". And from there a legal fight and vote recount got underway.

"They" claimed they found some hundreds of thousands of unsubmitted ballots just within the that single Florida county. No other county in the state has had so much controversy. If one were to do the math, that number of missing ballots, not only would have turned the governors race, but the added voter count was far in excess of the voters on file in that county. This is fraud of the worst kind, illegal in every sense of the laws we are suppose to be governed by. And yet, there was no prosecution of the wrongdoers. The rightful candidate for governor still won, but the democrats, under the leadership of Ms. Snipes in this case, tried every deception to sway the election.

In earlier campaigns, during the 2000 election cycle, she was accused of this same trick, controversy, of destroying ballots, missing ballots, and not removing ineligible voters from the roles. This is a crime against everything this country was founded upon, and crimes that were not investigated or prosecuted. The supervisor is to report results within 30 minutes after the polls close, and over 43 hours later, Broward and Palm Beach counties had not reported their legal results. It's all very fishy, and grossly dishonest. How is it that we allow these people to run elections, run our governing offices, and are given control over our lives?
The mail-in ballot is probably the single greatest area where one can cheat. Without any type of verification, "anyone" can submit a ballot mailer (as allowed by each state law). Nancy Pelosi,

Speaker of the House, has been strongly pushing for additional postal service funding, just in time for the 2020 presidential election. Under a provision of the 2020 Cares Act, such a funding for the post office would allow some 40 million (approximately) ballots to be mailed or collected by "canvassers". That person would then take the mail-in ballots to the post office for actual mailing. This is to avoid the voters from being out in public during the Covid-19 Chinese Plague. Sounds nice on paper, but the prospect for fraudulently altering the ballots is very real. There is factual evidence that such a ploy was planned (reported by Glenn Beck , on Blaze TV,8/20/20).

Throughout history, it is widely known that "dirty" politicians make promises they never keep, and do all sorts of pre-voting activities to manipulate the would-be voter. Some of the antics are "legal", others not so much, but that is what we expect from some politicians. Perhaps that is fine, before the vote, but to alter an election "after" the polling stations are closed is greatly different.

Whether any of these types of manipulations by one party or another are true of not, the point is that our free and open society is based upon an election system that is not tampered with. One of the great lures of why immigrants want to come to our shores is because of the free and fair election process. If the vote is tampered with, then the freedom of our election system, our core fundamental right, then no longer exists. We would be the same as every other totalitarian regime, Russia, China, Venezuela, Cuba, and so on.

BEWARE THE BLUE HATS

To be clear, if the new democrat party holds to the teachings and practices of socialistic ideals, then decide if electing those candidates aligns with your own values. What the democrat leaders want is power and control. They have, and will, beat down all opposition to this end, and that would not benefit Texas, or America.

Remember what Machiavelli said back around 1500, "Power corrupts, and absolute power corrupts absolutely". And examining history, even recent history, this is exactly true. When leaders get into power, unchecked by laws and constitutional limitations, then the mischief that resides in a mans' heart, festers into evil. Power is a drug, and intoxication that drives leaders mad, and ruins nations. The victims are the citizens. It is said that if a government is allowed to gain power (unchecked), then those leaders first abuse the power to their own gain. Then they oppress the people and silence opposition. And then, by historical fact, they mass murder their citizens. Do the research, it is the common pattern in every case.

"That can't happen in America. We have laws. We have three branches of government to limit power. We only elect good honest leaders." Too many people believe lies. Too many people have become brain-washed to the euphoria of promises made by candidates, unscrupulous elected leaders, and manipulated by a controlled media. Too many people have forgotten God, take responsibility for their own actions, and no longer can discern truth and right, from wrong.

As leaders are elected, they push laws and regulations to favor groups or individuals, or other self-serving ends, that can limit rights and privileges previously held. Elected leaders can fill the judicial branches with like-mind judges to twist or limit laws. Politicians can band together to halt or limit the good works and laws to govern the nation. Our constitutional government is a fragile system, threatened when corrupt leaders gain power. Although part of this is "normal" politics, swaying policies to favor a party platform, but we have seen this greatly limiting our rights and freedoms.

Over the past number of decades, individual rights and liberties have been greatly limited. Look at the laws relating to the Affordable Care Act (Obama Care), much of which was later found unconstitutional. Gun restriction laws, basically unconstitutional. "Hate Speech" laws and many of the antics in the public school system, is censorship. Freedom of Speech (and Religion), and the Right to Bear Arms are two areas have that been radically limited, far from the Framers original intent. If the right to bear arms is further degraded to the point where we can no longer protect ourselves and family, and, the ability to stand against a tyrannical government, then all other rights and freedoms will be lost. It is the right to protect yourself that assures we have all the other rights and freedoms. Take that away, by legal limitations, then beware the "Death Squads".

Never forget the Nazis. They were socialists with a national theme. They came to power in a time of crisis, offering promises and protection. "The more you help us fix and change the laws, the more we can provide for your needs". Laws changed, power consolidated, to the point where the private ownership of guns was banned. Guns for personal protection were outlawed and taken from the people. Without the ability to protect yourself or stand against unjust rulers, freedoms of speech and religious practices were taken from the people. More and more rights and freedoms were given up or taken away, to the point where Hitler became all powerful, pushing his personal agenda onto the nation and the world. How did that turn out for the citizens? How many millions, of their own citizens, did the government slaughter? Remember World War II? Is that still taught in our school system?

Along the same progression and results, the Russians under Stalin, murdered millions and millions of their own citizens who opposed his gain of power. The same scenario as with Nazi Germany, China, Cambodia, Venezuela, Cuba, and every other socialist nation. "A nation of laws, rights, and liberties, whittled away by leaders, then consolidating their power as given (or taken), leads to the death of the people, and ruin of the nation."

Not much is ever talked about Cambodia. Paul Pott, and the "Hitler youth-like Red Shirts", enforcing the dictates of the evil ruler. The Red Shirts suppressed opposition resulting in the death of millions of their own citizens. Remember the "Camaruge and the Killing Fields"? In every country, throughout Africa, South America, and Asia, where power is allowed to concentrate into the hands of a few rulers, abuse, oppression, and death follows. Every time, without fail, just study history. That is, if the history books are not re-written or burned to hide that reality.

The notion that socialism is "okay" or even good for a nation is absurd. It does not work, never has, never will. It can not, because "power corrupts, and absolute power corrupts absolutely". It has turned out disastrously for every nation since the dawn of man, and no rational way it can ever change. Human nature is that of lust, violence, and a thirst for power.

The difference with our nation, and our governmental structure, is God. America was founded with a Judeo-Christian belief, becoming the foundational stones of every law and thought written in the US Constitution. The leftists and educational elitists will deny that, and scream about some insane alternate reality, but fact is fact. If libraries still exist where books (the kind with ink and paper) still reside, one can research the writings of every founding father and framer of the document to read of their faith-based ideology. Is that a bad thing? The leftists of the democrat party would say so, because their agenda is different.

But America has lasted for over two hundred years, with the ideas that individual are good if not oppressed by rulers, and that man can do good works. Look at what America has done, created, built, fought for, stood against, the freedoms and liberties enjoyed, and so on. There is a lot of negative things that has happened over this time also. True, but the system of this government, for people to rise up and make positive changes for all, has prevailed. The American system of government, built on our religious premise, has worked for the health and happiness of all (or most anyways). The American system of a representative democracy is not perfect. We are flawed people, and sometimes we mess up. We can be greedy, hateful, self-servicing, and so on, but the government was designed to balance powers, which has worked pretty well until now.

Our system of government, protects the rights and privileges of the individual, not the State. We have the freedom to speak out against the government, and someone who wails against the goodness of our country, is also protected. Why change this? Why would any rational sober person think there is a better system to govern a nation? Apparently, the new democrat party sees it differently.

ABOUT LOSING OUR LIBERTIES

Is it possible to lose our Constitutional rights and freedoms? These are guaranteed under the law, aren't they? Yes, but no.

With each election, it results in more radical thinking politicians taking office, by which they get laws and regulations passed to silence free speech, for instance. Not so long ago, one could talk openly of another person or a group of people, have heated opposing debate, but that now is limited by "hate speech laws" and other controls. Yes, for sure it is not nice or kind to talk ill of another person or group, but can we not speak what's on our mind anymore? What if you spoke against a government agency or a governmental employee? Laws are being passed to limit what you can say against the government. What was accountability of government by the people, laws are starting to restrict that opposition, and then bring about serious consequences. The silencing of open discussion, debate, or defiance, is control of our liberty. Some politicians seek more control over us by enacting more laws and regulations in every area of our lives. Learn who the candidates are before you vote. Does the party platform, their set of ideals, align with your own, and how you want to live?

If democrat politicians (who have the mission to control the lives of the people) are elected, they will enact laws to reduce or eliminate the rights and privileges we hold, in particular our freedom to speak in opposition, our rights to bear arms, and so on. As we lose our freedom of speech (again as an example), we become slaves to the government.

Don't the republicans seek control also? Yes, sure they do, as all who are elected are subject to the lusts of power and control. It's just that in recent times, the democrat party has become so radical in their quest to control people by restrictive laws and regulations. Is that right or even fair? Some think it's fine, others are less happy, but the movement towards a socialist and totalitarian slavery will end the liberties and freedoms we still have.

This trend in our elections and the types of people elected to office is actually very scary. Too many are pushing for a government led, governmental controlled society. All countries that have embraced that style of slavery, are unproductive, with a people that are unhappy. Those nations, historically, have not remained very long.

OTHER FREEDOMS TO LOSE

Freedom to speak out and worship freely, are not the only rights and freedoms we can lose, but all of the others as well.

Gun rights are greatly threatened too. The Second Amendment protects the citizens' right to bear arms, for personal and family protection, but also to stand against tyrannical rulers. This fight has escalated in recent years, flamed by the biased media, and outspoken elitists. Here too, the critics claim that having guns is unsafe, yet those same individuals have armed security and walled homes.

We have plenty of good Gun laws in effect, but some are not adhered to in different states. Rather than add new laws to further restrict gun ownership, how about enforce the current laws? For example, the laws about background checks for gun purchasing was developed with the assistance of the NRA. The way it is suppose to work, is that criminal offenders are suppose to have their names and information submitted by the state and local levels into the NCIC (National Criminal Information Center) database, administered by the FBI. From there, everyone with access to the system can then approve or deny a purchase via the information submitted. Therein lies the rub. Information has to be submitted into the system, which is done at the state or and local levels. Not to do so, makes the whole background checking system incomplete due to the lack of relevant data. It is a good law and a good system, if it were used as intended.

Also, beware the "Red Hat" laws. Many states are implementing what is called Red Hat laws, whereby any person can accuse another person of being "dangerous". This then triggers local law enforcement to confiscate that accused persons' firearms. Based on merely hearsay, without proof, and without due process. Is that not a violation of many of our personal rights and freedoms? Yes, and it is yet another way the leftists are starting to "void" the Second Amendment. The gun owner is proven "guilty" until they can prove their innocence. That is the opposite of how how legal system is suppose to work.

What the democrats and the anti-gun activists keep calling for is gun control via regulations and restrictions. They also seek ever higher taxation on guns and ammo, which further restricts ownership. They are now openly pushing the idea of outright confiscation. Up until the 2020 election cycle, the democrats have kept "confiscation" out of any open discussion. Now, the party platform openly declares that it is on their agenda. Clearly, this is a violation of our rights that they will legislate around if they gain further control.

Would guns were taken away from the people, we would have a safer country, right? Only if you live in the same alternate reality the democrats and "gun-haters" The reality is, America is safer with the private ownership of guns. The media never reports the facts, but the FBI and any police precinct do show the stats of how many crimes are stopped before they happen, lives that saved, and personal property that is protected, from would-be "bad hombres". The media is in league with the democrat party to push a narrative that guns are bad (as well as the police, and white males).

As you look at the history of every nation that has turned socialist, the first thing the government would do is to remove the guns. Remove the ability of the citizens to fight against injustice, and the people will be easily controlled. Remove the guns, and all other rights and freedoms can not be defended. Again, take Nazi Germany for example. There was strong and active opposition to the rise of the national-socialists, but once the guns were seized, the Nazis eliminated all of the critics. And we are talking about the government killing its own citizens. Look at what happened in Russia, China, Venezuela, Cambodia, Cuba, and every other country that followed this path. And these people want to take away our right to defend ourselves? It is that scary.

Personal property rights and the "due process" of law, goes in lock-step with the seizure of our firearms. Again, under the "Red Hat" laws, if local law enforcement can break down your door in the middle of the night to seize your personal protection, that violates many of our rights guaranteed under the constitution. But they have the "right" by a piece of paper, and the unsubstantiated word of another person (that you would not have the right to face) to take your property? That is not the American way or the process we have lived for the last 200 years. These Red Hat laws open up all sorts of violations of our rights, and who is going to stop this?

Freedom of religious worship? Our Judeo-Christian roots that bore this country and our entire legal system, has been greatly under attack as well. We are free to worship whom and what we like, or nothing at all, without the interference of government mandating what we can do. But the attacks on our (Christian) beliefs, and how we are able to openly express that, is equally being censored and shut down.

The idea of "separation of Church and State", has been grossly portrayed by those seeking to abolish Christianity. Thomas Jefferson and Hamilton had written about this matter from the beginning, citing that "not separation, but rather that "government shall not impose a religion". In other words, government would not declare a State religion. Being a person of faith, whatever you believe, and part of the government structure, should not be an issue. But watching every Supreme Court nomination hearing, and even most Cabinet level screenings, there are those people, namely the democrats, that scream about the separation of Church and State. Having a person that holds a belief and moral compass in public office is a good thing. Look at the corrupt lying filth currently serving in office, and then decide which is better.

ABORTION IS LEGALIZED MURDER

Although abortion is not a right, it does relate greatly to our rights. And what about "the right to life"? The abortion question, is not just a freedom of religious worship, but it is also a freedom of speech. Perhaps the greater overall question is whether it is right and lawful for the government to kill, or sanction the killing, of its own citizens. Although the Supreme Court allowed the ability to kill unborn babies as a rule of law in Roe vs. Wade in 1973, is it right? No, it is a disgusting and abhorrence to everything good and honorable that this country touts to be. Murder is murder. An unborn child is still a human being, up until now. But, "by law", murder is no longer considered murder. The right of the woman to kill her unborn (or born child in some states), is "legally" up to her.

The State of New York, Virginia, and Vermont have passed new laws allowing the death of babies right up until the child takes its first breath. And, the voting assembly members applauded the new laws with resounding glee! It is said that liberty will die with resounding applause. Are we there? Whether life begins at conception or when a baby draws its first breath, is irrelevant. The question is, how can we as a nation allow the murder of our own innocent and defenseless citizens? We are suppose to be a nation ruled by law, but not all laws are good or just. Where is the sanity of our lawmakers? This is murder, plain and simple. Elections have consequences, and the people have voted for Death.

Now if this hennas debauchery of justice is not overruled, then the rights of free speech, religious worship, and "the pursuit of happiness", are made mute. Our freedoms as guaranteed under the US Constitution are destroyed. Those lawmakers, supporters of such legislation, and any group or organizations that adheres with such, are murders and co-conspirators. Is this country really going down this path? Then truth and justice in America is a lie!

What follows next? Well, because the murder of babies is made legal, the next step is to broaden that "definition" of whom can be (legally) murdered. Next will be young children no longer wanted by their parents, or perhaps the elderly will be killed at the whim of madmen. Then from there, any opposition group or segment of citizens, like white males, Christians, deplorable republicans, and so on, can face the death squads (by law). "When the sword is unsheathed, it is difficult to put it back without first spilling blood."

Here also, if and when the government is allowed to restrict your rights to own firearms, or takes them away completely, then there will be no more questions about religion, free speech, abortion, rights to assemble, protests against the government, property ownership, or anything else. Control of every facet of our lives is socialism, and it destroys a nation, study history. "Those who gain power will abuse it, then they will oppress the people, which then they will start murdering the citizenry." Strongly ponder these thoughts

A COUPLE FINAL THOUGHTS

If democrat politicians (who have the mission to control the lives of the people) are elected, they will enact laws to reduce or eliminate the rights and privileges we hold. We have been subject to this during the Obama years, and there is no chance the democrats will return to the Kennedy-era doctrine. The far left of the party has openly declared and embraced socialism and that does not sit well for our rights and freedoms. And fairly stated, any party or group (not just the democrats) has the desire to gain power and influence, that is our human nature. The point has been made clear, that the new democrat party are those seeking radical changes in the lives of every American.

In particular, our freedom to speak in opposition, our rights to bear arms, are gravely at risk. As we lose our freedom of speech (again as an example), we become slaves to the government. Power and control unchecked, will destroy a nation. Just watch and study for yourself what is happening all across Texas and the country, we are at war!

This trend in our elections and the types of people elected to office is actually very scary. Too many candidates, elitists, and segments of the population, are pushing for a government-led, governmental controlled society. Free health care, free schooling, free stuff, but it all has great costs. Nothing is free. All handouts from a public source, costs somebody something. It is usually from high taxation rates, but also through limits of free choice and decisions.

Our system of government was designed and set up to assure the people would have the liberty to become all they can aspire to do. The freedom of free and open speech has been the cornerstone of the greatness this country has shared, rooted in the process of free and open elections. Every vote counts, and every citizen has a duty to make this country better, according to their own conscience.

As our society writhes with turmoil and unrest, there are many issues to resolve for the greater good. And in this country, and for the 2020 election cycle, many groups are seeking to undermine our rights and liberties to vote, to have free and open speech, our ability to protect ourselves, and so on. It is critical for the survival of Texas, and the nation as a whole, to learn about the candidates before they get elected, and stand with those who think the same. This is no time for Texans to sit idle, the 2nd Alamo is near.

ABOUT THE AUTHOR

I grew up in a middle class family, had a father that worked, a mother that stayed home and raised children, the typical traditional American home. We had a small house, one car, (no) white picket fence, we had pets, regular schooling, church-goers, watched news and various TV shows, and had all of the cliche normal things in life typified during the 1950s and 60s. Life was normal and decent, reasonably peaceful, and safe.

My father was a veteran, worked a blue collar job, and was a straight-line democrat, just like his father before him. The Kennedy era thinking of party politics was pretty much his thinking as well. And for many decades, that seemed to work well in America. I too learned and adopted similar ideas of how life and government should work and coexist.

But that has changed radically over the past couple decades as the democrat party is no longer the party of the average working man. One would best describe the party as what we used to call the Communist-Socialist party during that earlier era. Now the party is all about hate speech, bigotry, division, dirty-politics, rampant dishonesty and deception by party leaders and candidates, and everything revolving around government control. This is no longer the democrat party America once loved.

The candidates and false narratives they promoted were enough to make me switch parties. Over the last many election cycles while the democrats drove further left, I pushed my family and friends to switch parties and vote further right. Not that the republicans are perfect by any means, but they do hold to more of the values and principles I do. The biggest area where they align with my own thinking are the ideas of limited government, a government hands-off ideology, and support of the Constitution and the foundations of this country. Upholding our rights and freedoms are more their forte, so this is where we will stay.

My hope is to share these thoughts with you, so that you can glean some insight of the struggle we face over our dying liberties. Thank you reading this.

Also consider these other books written about our Rights and Freedoms. These also are found on Amazon Kindle under the Politics section. Look for:

"The Democrat Blue Wave is the Zombie Apocalypse"
by T. H. Logwood
ASIN: B07MYBFKT1

*****

"In the Name of Jesus, Repent America!"
by T. H. Logwood
ASIN: B07NBXYLLB

*****

"The End of American Freedom"
by T. H. Logwood
ASIN: B07MSJ4QD7